Farewell and a Handkerchief

Poems from the Road

By Vítězslav Nezval

Translated from Czech by Roman Kostovski

Plamen
Press

Washington, DC

Plamen Press

9039 Sligo Creek Pkwy Suite 1114 Silver Spring, Maryland 20901

www. plamenpress.com

Published by Plamen Press, 2020

Printed in the United States of America

10 9 8 7 6 5 4 3 2 1

PUBLISHER'S CATALOGING-IN-PUBLICATION DATA

Names: Nezval, Vítězslav, 1900-1958, author. | Kostovski, Roman, 1968- translator.
Title: Farewell and a handkerchief : poems from the road / Vitezslav Nezval ;
[translated by] Roman Kostovski.
Description: Silver Spring, MD: Plamen Press, 2020
Identifiers: LCCN 2019949970 | ISBN 978-0-9960722-5-0 (paperback)
Subjects:
LCSH: Czech poetry--Translations into English.
Czech poetry--20th century. | Surrealism--Czechoslovakia.
Avant-garde (Aesthetics)--Czechoslovakia. | Experimental poetry.
BISAC: POETRY / European / General.
Classification: LCC PG5040.24.E9813 F37 2020 (print)
LCC PG5040.24.E9813 (ebook) | DDC 891.8/6--dc23.

Translated from Czech by Roman Kostovski

Edited by Rachel Miranda Feingold

Cover Art by Adolf Hoffmeister (used with permission)

Cover Design by Roman Kostovski

Editor

Rachel Miranda Feingold

To Jarmila, who loved Nezval like she loved the Spring

Table of Contents

Foreword

Karen von Kuneš

Yale University

Few nations love poetry as much as Czechs do. In this respect, one of the most prolific and beloved poets, Vítězslav Nezval (1900-1958), goes hand-in-hand with French surrealist André Breton, a creator of the first *Manifeste du Surréalisme* in 1924. Several years later, Nezval translated Breton's surrealist manifesto into Czech and published it in Prague. The French word *surréalisme* was actually coined by a fierce defender of cubism and forefather of surrealism, the French poet of Polish descent, Guillaume Apollinaire.

Apollinaire's poem "Zone," in which he describes Paris sensorially—traversing time and space—left a lasting impression on Czech poets, particularly on Nezval. Milan Kundera wrote that Apollinaire "stood front and center of global literary history as seen from twentieth-century Prague,"[1] and Nezval proclaimed that it was Apollinaire's "chimerically veiled eyes" that taught him to see Prague and its tales in a different light. It was this discovery, this reinvention of Nezval's perception, that shaped the way he subsequently approached his subject, be it Prague, the cities of Europe, or everyday objects and happenings.

Nezval's close friendship with both André Breton and Paul Éluard was instrumental in establishing "The Czech Surrealist Group" in 1934 with its journal *Surrealismus,* of which he became the chief editor. It is important to note that this was the first formal surrealist art group outside of France. As a cultural and art movement, reflected both in prose and poetry and in the visual arts (predominantly paintings, but also film and sculpture), surrealism plays with dreams, imagination, abstract and incongruous images; in one word, it plays with the subconscious, which can often be suppressed in real

---

[1] Derek Sayer, *Prague, Capital of the Twentieth Century: A Surrealist History* (Princeton: Princeton UP, 2013), pp. 64-5.

life. Like André Breton, Nezval attempted to combine the abstract elements of the unreal (fantasy, superstition, dreams, etc.) into one kind of supreme reality. This style of freedom and spontaneous creativity are reflected in his uniquely Czech style of naturally flowing rhythms and rhymes in his book of poems, *Sbohem a šáteček*, or *Farewell and a Handkerchief*, presented by Plamen Press in this superbly poetic English translation by Roman Kostovski.

While many readers might never have heard of Vítězslav Nezval or of other noted Czech surrealists and poets such as Karel Teige, Jindřich Štyrský, Josef Šíma, Toyen (a woman poet whose real name was Marie Čermínová), or Jaroslav Seifert (the Nobel Prize winner for poetry in 1984), it is crucial to realize that much artistic and scientific creativity came from this country, known today as the Czech Republic. It is a country that, for over seventy years, was united with Slovakia into Czechoslovakia, and prior to that had a turbulent history which continued throughout the twentieth century. For instance, the founder of psychoanalysis, Sigmund Freud, whose famous *The Interpretation of Dreams* (1899) largely influenced the surrealist movement, was born in Moravia—today the eastern region of the Czech Republic; however, in the nineteenth century it was a territory of the Austro-Hungarian Empire. Other influential figures to which Moravia (in Czech *Morava*) gave birth are the phenomenologist Edmund Husserl; the first president of Czechoslovakia, Tomáš Garrigue Masaryk, a philosopher who married American Charlotte Garriguethe; well-known composer Leoš Janáček; the preeminent novelist Milan Kundera; the secession painter Alfons Mucha (whose status equals Gustav Klimt's and Egon Schiele's); and German industrialist Oskar Schindler, who is credited with saving twelve hundred children from being sent to concentration camps during the Holocaust. This category of outstanding creators born in Moravia could be substantially enlarged, and the poet and playwright Vítězslav Nezval should be placed on the top of the ladder. In 1932, he hosted the largest exhibition of surrealist art of the 1930s in the Prague gallery Mánes. Works by Czech surrealists figured prominently, along with works of internationally recognized artists such as Salvador Dalí, Joan Miró, Paul Klee, and Max Ernst.

If Vítězslav Nezval has gone largely unrecognized outside of the Czech Republic, there are valid but unfortunate political and linguistic reasons. The country went through a number of political upheavals during Nezval's time: World War I; the dissolution of Austro-Hungary in 1918, replaced by an independent but short-lived democratic republic due to its annexation to Germany during the Nazi invasion in 1938; and after World War II, the arrival of the Communist regime in 1948, and the country's subsequent enclosure behind the Iron Curtain for the next forty years. These political changes prevented Western scholars from researching Czech culture or from mastering Czech, a lexically and morphologically rich and beautiful but difficult language, which itself created a barrier to reading, understanding, and enjoying the melodic verses of Nezval and many other marvelous Czech poets.

In the early 1920s, together with Karel Tiege, Nezval formed a purely Czech avant-garde group, Devětsil ("Nine Forces"), a poetic gathering with the flavor of dadaism, cubo-futurism, and constructivism joined by such talented artists as Jiří Wolker, Konstantin Biebl, and Jaroslav Seifert. The resulting literary form of poetism, or *poetismus* in Czech, was meant to celebrate the people's art (the art of the proletariat) and to make it accessible to everyone. In this spirit, poetism propagated sensual pleasures combined with an exploration of daily tasks and consciousness in order to establish a new art of everyday life, elevating it into a state of *poesis*, as the critic Bronislava Volek named it. A narrow bridge connected the two movements: poetism, which sought to unite art and life, evolved naturally into surrealism, a unifier of dreams and reality. Representative works of Nezval's poetism are in his collection, *Abeceda*, poems beginning with each letter of the alphabet, as well as playful, mischievous, and occasionally quirky ones with a multitude of themes including eroticism: *Podivuhodný kouzelník* (1922) or *The Marvellous Magician*, and *Akrobat* or *Acrobat* (1927).

But the collection of poems that Czechs love the most is *Sbohem a šáteček, Farewell and a Handkerchief*, here introduced to English-speaking lovers of poetry for the first time. These poems are Nezval's reflections from his travels in 1933 to Paris, Avignon, Vienna, the Alps, Monaco, Méditerranée, Cannes, and Italy, including Venice and Napoli (Naples). He attempted to integrate everything he came into contact with, achieving a heightened sense of perceptive and imaginative reality. The collection is framed by the motif of a handkerchief, first appearing as a symbol of sadness while he was departing from his native land, "Today I'm leaving on the brink of tears," and reappearing at his return home from "magic" lands, once again to "tearfully admit my pain." However, travels also gave him a deep joy, and while the reader experiences the sense of sorrow, or in Czech, the feeling of *litost*—the kind that Milan Kundera masterfully described in *The Book of Laughter and*

Forgetting—Nezval's *lítost* is effervescent, joyful and positive. His return marks his thirty-third birthday, a significant milestone in his life. In this collection, the reader comes across unique associations, occasionally of hallucinating effects, but often presented in loving detail, and seen through the eyes of an innocent and yet thoroughly experienced admirer of the everyday. Nezval's poetic mind creates an evocative imagery of cities, countries, people, social reality of the rich and the poor, the good and the bad (such as approaching Nazism) in a stream of harmonic rhyming. The intentionally lacking punctuation creates a sense of unity of the world which surrounds him and which reminds him of existential reality, as in: *Věř když se láska poláme jak hračka je lépe nechat ji*. "When love is broken like a porcelain dove/Just let it go!"

The last stanzas of the volume have become a credo for Czechs—they are reflected in songs, recited by school children, and quoted by young adults and old folks alike. It is precisely this simple beauty of life that Czechs admire in their beloved poets, and in Nezval in particular:

> *Farewell, and if we no longer meet*
> *Our time was marvelous—we've shared enough*
> *Farewell, and soon our trysts will be*
> *With someone new, someone else's love*

Farewell and a Handkerchief

Poems from the Road

The Pocket Handkerchief

The Pocket Handkerchief

Today I'm leaving on the brink of tears
Handkerchief in pocket, a moment to grieve
If the world were a poster I'd no longer care
I'd tear it down cynically and toss it in the sea

A valley of tears swallowed me like a whale
My poster map folded in thirty-odd places
Forgive me oh lark, as always I fail
Whenever I weep, my sorrow is graceless

The handkerchief flutters, it unveils cities
Waving grotesquely out of a tunnel
Too bad that death is not just a journey
From where I'd wake in an unknown hotel

And you who loves like Andrea del Sarto
Surrender your silk to those womanly eyes
And if death is a whirlwind, an instant, a somersault
Don't spin just yet! Hail, hawks in the skies!

Poetry

Breeze, oh breeze! I licked my fingertip
To know the point from which you blow
Oh breeze! I'll gather what you sow
Breeze! I have filled my grip

Soul, you cat! Stretch your back!
The breeze wishes to fondle you
And sparks, oh, I can hear you crack
In ways the crickets never do

I'm sowing larvae in the moss
And lightning, the fire of rain
Oh breeze! What will you sow again?
I'll sow, I'll sow only solace

Dowry

Everyone loves that land
Where they leaped over milestones
My highlands you made me
The vagrant I am

Everyone loves that time
When they believed in ghosts
The dragonfly mostly
Brings these voices to mind

Everyone loves a world
Clothed in darkness
As I love those old dresses
Of nineteen-oh-five

The Border

Don't sit, little bird, on that vibrating saw
Fly away! It'll destroy you like a storm
Don't sit, little bird, on that border stone
Too many await you en route to the Nile

The bird sits on that blade and refuses to go
Nations here once guillotined each other
The bird answers only to Nature his mother
Is he German? Lithuanian? Who needs to know?

I envy you, bird, I envy your flowerbed
Your Socratic philosophy
As I sit by sweet Thaya's stream
Amid the odor of sulfur and bayonets

Vienna

One Sunday at five in the afternoon
I walked alone by the Schönbrunn
And the sun released its golden crown
On the highest column of that remnant
Of glory nearly doomed
On the highest column of that remnant
Of glory already doomed
On the highest column of the palace Schönbrunn
That Sunday at five in the afternoon

And it gleamed like a cathedral's monstrance
A golden monstrance that appears in dreams
Emerges, and how terrifying it seems!
More horrid than a treasure in a casket
More frightful than a treasure in a casket
It appeared before me like in a dream
A gleaming gothic and liturgical monstrance

And in its jewels I saw the eyes of maids
Eyes of servant girls born in the highlands
And smoking wicks in midnight bed lamps
Eyes like ribbon colors, eyes along with braids
Blue, green, purple ribbons along with braids
Worn at home in the Czech lands
Eyes of young and cheerful Bohemian maids

Oh that sparkling white elephant-shaped spine
The spine of that monstrance I had come to dread
With a sigh I sadly shook my head
How many tens and hundreds combined?

How many thousands have fallen combined
To uphold that spine I had come to dread
That sparkling white elephant-shaped spine?

That Sunday at five in the afternoon
When I walked alone by the Schönbrunn
I cursed that imperial golden crown
And all those crowns that looked the same
I cursed them all and wished them the same
That down they'd fall like the court of Schönbrunn
That Sunday at five in the afternoon
One Sunday at five in the afternoon

Ringstrasse

A larva shows her naked belly
While flashing her gaudy trinkets
Greenflies and more greenflies above me
Relish the lasting silence

The lamp winks dandily
At the humid street
Greenflies, *c'est la vie*
Fancy Death, cover your belly!

The Alps

Oh enemy of pathos and lithographs of cows
I dread those prayers that smell of kitsch
I've dreamt on a sandpile for thirty years now
But I won't submit easily to those glorious peaks

I fear these Danaans and the gifts they bear
My sandpile was swept away by the wind
I've seen hundreds of Trafalgar-like squares
I've drunk many a lover's and killer's poisons

The tearful climate corrupted my eyes
A weathered frigate threw me about
I lived like a castaway climbing up a hillside
Cleaned and soiled by a handful of clouds

Playfully I gazed upon the tourists
Who'd prefer a crutch to a palace key
A labyrinth to a royal court or a bust
An elephant to a minuscule flea

In this cage of meridians I took my seat
Like a gelding with blinders, I've travelled these Alps
I'm off to greet those burlesque chimney sweeps
Who on New Year's Day wear their white caps

And when this airy hattery filled my senses
A fragrant smoke covered the horizon
Were thieves of magma pits playing with frankincense
Or have we passed a recent battle zone?

Roaring white clouds like Socrates's hair
Became a mirror in the twilight rain
Old man's wisdom, you remember that era
When a heart like mine was a lively flame.

Back then mongers of stars played games
Don't be shy Byron! Come watch us if you like!
How do the Alps look from a plane?
Pilots, how do you view those flyspecks in white?

I thought of the wisdom and grace of old age
Its silvery flow like the streams in the Alps
I thought of a future where liars lose praise
Where pride is not measured by seizing a scalp

I thought of a peace where the threads of machines
Rip in a race to feed hungry crowds
At the alpine hotels with their lavish cuisines
The last of the gluttons are forced to check out

The unbridled twilight crimsoned these highlands
Then quietly faded in the morning meadows
I listened to the bubbling of shallow backwaters
Along with their sapphires, along with their sparrows

Behold the vertigo of monuments for no one
In a wind scented by many kinds of mallows
What moved me the most was the leg of a cold nun
Rigidly resting out of her shadows

The redheaded herdsmen up on the hillsides
Cleave to an udder in the afternoon breeze
In vertigo they breath the scent of old mandrakes
Grown from the matter of their very own seeds

Vastness expanded over the mountains
The frightened horizon cowered piously
I could see lizards and I could see cow heads
My apocalypse transpired too rapidly

I came across a strange little goose maid
Herding white pillows on pastures to feast
Conquered by tenderness and love in its cradle
I'd sacrifice my life for all of her geese

By a blue cave of metaphysical neckties
Under a hillside of accordions never played
I rode the express train as I waved my goodbye
To a moldering old castle vanishing in the haze

Like colophony in a pot, the night thickens too soon
The evening ripens through the worm-shaped tunnels
Artificial lakes, artificial dreams, and moons
Quietly swing on the leaves of asphodels

Boulders blasted out of slaughterhouse craters
Crush strange emotions I've never felt before
Nature here blesses its own Easter Friday
Where martyria embrace these teardrops of stone

Oh enemy of pathos and lithographs of cows
I dread those prayers that smell of kitch
I've dreamt on a sandpile for thirty years now
And I won't submit easily to those glorious peaks

And yet the Stone Age through which I slither
Upon this winding serpentine road
despite the ashes and despite the steel
It crushes more than those carpets hold

Those carpets on which I fly through my life
A life with chimneys where civilization rises
And yet, born in the thicket, the edelweiss
Has more life than our own native irises

Smoked-out lungs and parched edelweiss
Will never conquer tuberculosis
Moldering edelweiss isn't bothered by greenflies
Nature numbs me in a cloud of narcosis

And it isn't just a cheap miserly drug
For which I pay with a morning migraine
My soul is fresh like Augustus's toga
Fluttering windward at the arena stage

Arriving in Paris

The French Customs Officer

Hey player! Change your play!
It has such weak and shallow rules
Is this compartment a dressing room
For the French ballet?

"Madame, your dress
Awakens doubt inside me
With my verification of your chastity
You'll soon reach home and rest."

His nostrils discern
The smell of clothing and covers
Of maidens, mothers, and lovers
And then calmly he returns

To his bachelor's cell
Where in his bed he sleeps well

Awakening by a Fountain

He who fights tooth and nail with sleep
Usually surrenders
to the first breeze
Like your restless curly hair

He who fights tooth and nail with death
In the end will bind
With his final breath
Like a statue and ivy vines

I battle the sleep of death by waking
I sleep like smoldering hay
But somene is forcing me
To plunge into disarray

Someone is poking my pupils
with needles; pestering me now
When my eyelids are feeble
Pulling strands from my innocent brows

Is it me? No, it's just a grain of sand
A barge swaying in a trance
On a fountain of flowers
And morning rays in France

No, it's a ball pierced with pins
That sleeps and then lightly rises
Through the air with a scent of mint
Golden needles from a summer fountain

And it is I who remind the kings
Of their famous rides towards Versailles
Where the stars in the mornings fade
And then finally they subside

Arriving in Paris

Oh how disappointing are the cities we dream about!
I confess to those towers that called me here
And blindly, oh Paris, I slide through your mouth
And kneel before you, oh fair Sacré-Cœur

Now I'm embraced by hundreds of doors
With a heartfelt yawn Paris welcomes me
Frankly, oh Paris, I expect nothing more
No need to change. I won't force you to be

Like that woman who deceived her man
By sculpting herself into his own illusion
Your silvery gray, your Cinderella skin
Leads me on like Medusa's own vision

You were Medusa when I dreamed about you
Now here I stand, a vagrant in prime
And the smallest bit that you're able to give
Lulls me to sleep like a drinking man's wine

Oh Paris! I won't deface you with a mask
Laugh out loud! Shout! Make haste!
To capture your passion is all that I ask
Along with that special spicy fish taste

The Square by the Stock Exchange

The square by the crippled stock exchange
Touts its past glory in this modern age
But as I see it, it's just a prop on a stage

God abandoned this vehicle along with its drivers
Dragging those busloads of ages
To that noisy garage of the stock exchange

I prefer chauffeurs and their unique roar
as they gamble near the taproom counters
I once saw one of them fly out a door

Go hang yourselves, gentlemen, or fight for your change
And whatever is left of your antiquated cult
On that beautiful square by the stock exchange

Rue de Richelieu

Greetings, Your Eminence!
Could I bend your ear, by chance?
Your street is long
Like a poet's desperate song
Take me please
To a room with more couches
Than bedbugs and fleas

Hôtel de Bretagne

The Hôtel de Bretagne has tapestry
That resembles the magic of old bonbonnières
My bed for two and a smell of pastry
Brought in by the servant Pierre

You old man with Biscot's[1] head
Uncle to ladies of Parisian streets
Did a harlot lay in my double bed?
Will she too disturb my sleep?

Which bedside does a man prefer?
Which a woman? Do you know?
Wait, don't tell me! Let me guess.
They change sides as they come and go.

With whom do you trade your fantasy,
And collect it with a guilty heart?
I might pay with my sanity
When I'm locked behind iron bars

---

[1] *Translator's note*: Georges Biscot was a French actor known for his awkwardly shaped head.

By the Palais-Royal

The Palais-Royal exposes its glory
Along with the charm of old hovels
A curious stranger walks by and dozes
Oh black ages, oh gray ages
The sky into the river changes
And everything in time will fade
As this prop upon its stage

Traffic Rules

At this carnival's gigantic shooting range
The traffic officer shouts Halt!

Oh how beautiful are these dead automobiles
If Pompeii were awake, it would have their appeal
And then their horns feel vibration
And in seconds a resurrecting sensation

At this carnival's gigantic shooting range
The traffic officer shouts Halt!

Rosé

Out of love for innocence
I drink this pink wine
And those who detest its flavor
Never experienced its intensity
Or the secrets it savors
Or its purity
You're a medieval painting with golden rays
When I drink you my bottle becomes a vase
I'd serve you to a sixteen-year-old maid
Who paints hearts on her cheeks playing roguish games

Longing

I felt a longing in this miraculous city
A longing for you, my dearest friends
Perhaps a good sleep will show me mercy
and my sorrow too will have an end

I felt a longing for you, my father
Or for you, my mother. If only I knew
I felt a longing for something random
I felt a longing out of the blue

Avenue de Maine

Your hand is dressed in a chimney sweep's glove
Every shop forms a bracelet
Coal and wine
Not a single movie sign
With the dirt under your nails
You point to Montrouge
And yet, poor girl, you smell of rouge

Rue de la Gaîté

Monsieur, come to my stand
Buy a button, take your pick
We'll have time for song and dance
And that thing there is for the flics[2]

My François is in a hole
I meant to say in La Santé
My François is an animal
But you can be my man today

Monsieur, poets are like simple boys
Buy my beads, would you please?
And we can have a week of joy
The hearts of women never ease

François will soon return
And Jeanette will cry once more
Aren't you just a bit concerned?
An Apache is your solemn foe

Monsieur, we'll laugh together
If you come tomorrow night
You'll notice I am quite clever
And *that* François doesn't like

Perhaps he's like every beau
Name me one who won't cut you down
Monsieur, why don't you buy my rose?
At midnight I'll be closing down

---

[2]*Translator's note:* "Flics" is the colloquial French name for the police.

Closerie des Lilas

Hail to the suitor of Black Venus!
He clears the cloudy water
As dusk arrives
Funerals without drums and parades
Mannequins without souls
In the windows forever turning halfway
Their fingernails competing with the stars
While Charles Baudelaire in the form of a cat
Watches as I write
Verses silent and then more silent
The classical wagon overturns
And dawn arrives
Packages of maximum tension
Ripened dreams at Closerie des Lilas
Burn in the little lamps like spodium
I don't need to smoke opium
Our dreams evaporate at minimal heat
And all of you without a fire
Come warm yourselves at this café
With a stove close to the street and a singing aperitif

By the Wall of Montparnasse Cemetery

By the wall of Montparnasse cemetery
I once stopped and then quickly walked by
I didn't go in. I didn't think to try

There lies the author of *Flowers of Evil*
So carry on
And hail this king who is long gone

My dear poet
If your fragile ears were still alive
You would hear daily
Your poems, and then your poems, and then your poems
In a thousand variations
Wouldn't it drive you insane?
Death is not the greatest evil
Either I'll go deaf from your chatter, sparrows
Or I'll find a door through which I can disappear!
Today I don't care
Today I can't hear
My dear poet
It was difficult back then as it is now
To revive a petrified tongue

Monument to Alfred de Musset

To be exhausted after thirty years
Is the task of great lovers
Or perhaps of those
Who waited too long to leave
One another.
Exhausted, he dies of lust
For the diamond that destiny never refined
He who had played a sovereign upon its bevels
Now stands baffled over the tempting stone
In front of this nothingness
He has lost the skill that once brought him fame
He hasn't the courage to be laughed at
As a beginner
By a woman without heraldry and title
Rather he stages impotence
For that famous courtesan whom he despises
And so, disgusted, with the diligence of a pupil
He polishes several more stones
On his pitiful little monument

Between Two Arcs de Triomphe

On Carousel Square
Allegorical venuses take the reins of a rather
Unique equipage
It's the Louvre
Let us take a ride
In that moving carriage
      hauling mythology from around the world

We shall relay in the Tuilleries
The statues run off and wander through the vast park
Playing hide and seek with the children
Sinking their toy ships in the ponds

Enormous silence that sleeps in the trees
An orchestra
And the leaves are falling
This scattered promenade is so beautiful

I knew a woman
Who was like the Tuilleries
Her lace, her bed, her evenings
Fell unconscious and her fingertips like the leaves
      shaken by the wind
Would excite old hopes within me

If only I had met you a little farther down
     on Union Square
Three or four years ago
So much courtship I would have rendered there

Today I am not the same

Farewell you flowers of the past
 I decipher picturesque calligraphy on an obelisk

And the fountain in the round center pool
Treats me to the taste of music
                                        by Claude Debussy
It is a fulfilling music school
That embraces calligraphy

Devoid of memory I sit here with joy
And I yield to this diamond circle
As I greet you, Elysian Fields
You enormous garland
Decorated with different flowers and different rays
We'll have lunch together at the cabaret
Where its batwings will lend us a piece of the night
 Or should we devour the mixed grills
Of trees, klaxons, and women's faces
In that royal equipage
Rushing underneath the great Arc de Triomphe
So that we can greet the star of stars?
Greetings, Étoile!

Rond Point des Champs-Élysées

From your bowls we drink your morning brew
Fountains of azure blue
Where has Titian gone away?
He was summoned to the Champs-Élysées

Les Grands Boulevards at Night

The freshly painted peacock upon Avenue de l'Opéra
                                        renders his fiery span
His hundredth and first head
Shrieks through the megaphones of Haussmann
                                        Boulevard
Paris lost that particular gem
On its way to Boulevard des Italiens

And all the cafés roll into the street

The paint suddenly changes
Into women, into restaurants, into cinemas

His voice continues to gripe
Like an old chasseur in the casinos

I hear you, creature of the Senegal
Your song resonant, like little cafés with tobacco
Glittering between the sounds of automobile
                                        horns
A raspy old harlot sings it once more

Will you announce the beginning of this fashion show
Introducing the hats of apaches and the legs of
                                        movie stars
In the same fashion as exploding parfumeries?

A ballet of policemen
Their automatic pistols
Beckon their automobile eyes
And the beautified brows of ladies
Carry the taste of sparkling pastels

The freshly painted peacock
In the storage room of the Opéra
Spreads out in a series of coulisses
Comes through the trapdoor to decorate the revue
On les Grands Boulevards at night

The First Quarter Moon Above Printemps

From this golden slipper
Venus's leg was born
Now which bottle should I barter
To conjure a stocking or a garter?

At the Louvre

At the Louvre

1

If a quick today will not give you satisfaction
Perhaps tomorrow will, or the day after, or somewhere
                            on another star in morningtime
The future is long, the days grow shorter
You will never return, your voice will return
When a wandering echo snatches it in morningtime
Perhaps tomorrow, or the day after,
                   or somewhere on another star

2

Woven Assyrian baskets!
I'd never want
to cause fear like a mummy
Give me the grace of shades on window frames

When they go out of fashion
They never shame

If you find them in a museum
Among the crush of many antiquities like me
It's refreshing, like a vent, like clean air
                                    like clear water

3

Oh, pebblestones!
A wave is the most gentle sculptor
The Egyptians knew this:
To give a stone complexion
There must be great love for life
For its sheep, for its twilight, for its maidens
Please, lamp
Revive my memories of those long gone.

4

This young man of Michelangelo's
Must have thrown himself into the sea every morning
The urge to be embraced by someone gave rise
to his well-rounded thighs
A young girl will see him as the brother
                                to whom she gives her chastity
His unfinished head is a guarantee
                                of a lasting lifespan
Bashful young man
All rests in the promise
Never to render a face
Dispassionately

5

To introduce harmony between the blue sky
The green landscape and a woman
Is a task for Botticelli's brush
Only rare summer days can do him justice

If their lips are like the the mountain springs
Then kiss and kiss them on the meadows
Oh arms, oh women
Oh moon!

6

Our sense of beauty often puts us to sleep
Eyes illuminate the moment in a drop of rain
While our entire lives are separated from us
     like a bolted cellar
I have already smoked so many cigarettes
That their taste has merged with the color gray
But in this instant I am moved by a musty smell
And I no longer know where I stand, in which place,
     in how many eras
All the chairs of my life have left me forsaken
And are present here in this seat
    which I have currently taken
In the center of this bizarre room made
    of twenty rooms
Only this sort of Realism truly fulfills me
Like the disemboweled cow of Rembrant van Rijn
Or the Samaritan no less disturbing
    no less genuine
I stand in front of a single court and I am everywhere
Like an inebriated alcoholic
Who falls into the embrace of a woman with
A hundred arms
Or the man to whom agony renders
A complete portrait of his life
Nothing disturbs me now
Not even wings or twilight
Or a festive afternoon with banners
Like the final judgment of all things
    awakened in a playful chimney

Every stroke of Rembrandt's brush
Defines a fully-formed pattern
And when a young novice painter
                              creates a replica
 He stuggles to emulate the character of that unique style
Oh aesthetics, I have not found you
Very likable, yet you are capable
Of satisfying beings who crave reality
This canvas made of angels, of aprons
                        and the color of molded walls
This canvas, this hypnotic canvas
Contains the present and the past and that
                    of which I know nothing at all

7

Some people reveal the whole truth
By cleverly keeping it covered
You, Picasso
The eyes of the woman I love thrill me most
When I walk by the windows and smell the drying shellac
When I listen to the most beautiful of operas
Alone behind closed curtains on a red
Plush chair

Flea Market

Flea Market

1

On Sunday out by Clignancourt Gate
The merchants' tents are pitched and draped
The flea market opens
On Sunday afternoon
Parisian fleas, come out of your rooms!

2

An old lamp, a mirror, candleholders
A woman tattooed from her fingers to her shoulders
She's decked out like a pretty page
All we need now is a circus stage

3

Monsieur, when that old usurer Goblec sucked you dry
Hardly a single thing remained
Just an old missal, withered and left behind

4

Louis Bonapart's chambermaid
Once lived in this salon
And soon when the tables turn
Your ministry chairs with their fancy linen
Will be perfect for our playful children

5

The veteran's leg
Is extremely solid
And his only shoe
Comes in handy when he's out to beg

6

My grandfather was a great reader of books
Why don't you buy his old glasses?
And on this sofa have a look!
Time quickly passes
You'll never need a radio

7

Brightly painted paravan
Dragging a parade of caravans
If you wish to be a traveler
You must learn it in your childhood

8

In those months spelled with Ju...
Take two
Or more seashells
While you're still offered a sea
Life is as uneasy as currency

9

Those who have rubbish should bring it
To my door
Poetry without rubbish can be a bore
The things that have passed through this garbage bin
That sou is older than a groschen
In France I've noticed everywhere
That poetry is an étagère

10

A louse with a candleholder for a head
A louse with the belly of a featherbed
Compares to an orchid in my fantasy
My dream is a flea market at its best
And I am happy among its chairs and pests

11

And finally we visit
                   only courtyards that seem unique
There stands a mill
I listen with passion to its terrifying
Dialogue

And so we study each other
Without pause, like a poem with the souls of readers
Our rendezvous
Chaotic, like flea market shopkeepers
End somewhere beyond the walls of innocence.
No, a life of obligation is a cross I'll never bear

Moulin de la Galette

The Magic of Montmartre

At Montmartre after Sunday
You can still get what you want
But you know today's blue Monday
Bad for business, to be blunt

The old houses on the hill
Grumble and growl as well
When the church of Sacré-Coeur
Passes by the gate to hell

The pubs on Place du Tertre
Tearful like young Werther
Beckon us to come their way
As if it were a Saturday

No one will make you laugh
Like the folks at Frightened Calf
Dance and song and jongleurs play
Till four o'clock come and stay

Montmartre's flag is rough
But it rises high like a seraph
Sprung from its humble means
It hails to its only queen

Its queen is Moulin de la Galette
She can't be younger than two hundred
A mill that no longer grinds
Despite those days in her prime

As I stand here at her door
Watching Paris from Sacré-Cœur
I can see as far as Chartre
Farewell, magical Montmartre!

Place du Tertre

My love, perhaps we both shall meet
When finally the world agrees
To sit together chair to chair
On that one Parisian square

Sacré-Cœur

Lonely white lady
You rival a steel tower
If I ever slander you, then call me a liar
And if I ever praise you
Let it be said that this poet escaped
That lasting gaudiness
Which makes him adore
Spotted circus drapes
Gaudy old tower, I don't need to speak
When all of Paris kneels at your feet

Lapin Agile

In the belly of the rabbit
That swallowed these holy frescoes
It is terrifying and it is pleasant
But what a shame, what great sorrow
That your visitors (from Wilde to Apollinaire)
Didn't come yesterday and won't come tomorrow.
And so instead of a festive toast
I drink from their unfinished goblets

Moulin de la Galette

Nothing will make me turn
Not even your eyes when your desires burn
Or your arms stretched windward and severed
Not even love, that minuscule token
That token always damning and revealing
But that time your heart was broken
You told me no, it was not for giving
Nothing will make me turn
Not even your eyes when your desires burn

The Bridge above Montmarte Cemetery

Our bus rushed onto the extended bridge
Of your hallucinations
You loved and you hated and this will never change
You loved and you died and this will never change
Just one more hallucination
Bridge of thirty stories

A May Day in Paris

A beautiful sky above that beautiful lament
A raspy old fife sings out while passing by
I follow that honeybee
                    to the Sara Bernhardt Theater
Where it disappears, and with it your youthful prime

It's the month of May
And not a single curtain can cover this trance
Not even my memories or Paris
                    or a single corner in France
And so I walk all the way to Cité
To Notre-Dame, that two-armed candleholder without candles
And the darkness of the empty church absorbs me
Its invisible lilacs continuously smoldering
With a smoke that slithers low above the ground

And then I remember nothing more

I awake on Boulevard Saint-Michel
                            near Muséa Cluna
And never notice the Chinese restaurant opening for me
Where puppet-like faces sleep
        And the spices fiercely place me under narcosis
Tea with the taste of blue
I seize a curtain, trembling, and like a lunatic I go
                            and sit down
A black student has just returned
                            from the Latin Quarter

My new friend then departs with a camera
                            heading for a hunt
The Parisian jungle with panthers built from books

A medical bulldog, a theological python
A little pooch that is so lyrical
                         it almost makes me blush
These pictures and years have since long withered away
                         yet not nearly as much as me
They are minuscule chronicles, each one remarkable

Saint Michael leads me by the hand
Where Rue Monsieur le Prince begins
A strange old man catches my eye
He nods at me and I don't know why

As if I were being pushed
I start walking at a faster pace
I don't know whether it is a tram or a fly
                         unpleasantly buzzing in my ear
I don't know whether it is a tram or a fly
But when I enter the Luxembourg Gardens
                         the old man is sitting nearby
Then my consciousness evaporates completely
And I have a letter to write
Fountains and children and balls and myself alone
Myself and a beautiful sky above that beautiful lament

I get carried away by the knee of a young governess
                         and I see with her eyes
A hawthorn at the feet of a marble angel
And if I don't realize her hopes by sunrise
I will be sad, I will be truly sad

Dressed in lace, I absorb the freshness of that leg
                         which incites me
And all of Luxembourg answers my plea
                         with your bosoms marshaled in a parade

The trees are rising, the fountain sings again
Its praline symphony
Like arms, my route welcomes me and pushes me away
And that small, uncertainly dressed old man is still there
Neither kings nor today's fashion
Could amaze me more
Than the breeze that whistles from the neighboring pavilion
Without knocking I enter the bedroom
                          with no ceiling and no walls
In the bedroom or rather in the bed
                          where you rest, Marianna!
I take off your leather gloves
Old man
And on this day my heart has to get over
                          many a varied wonder
It begins on the Rue Saint-Jacques
                          quite close to the observatory
An innocent coincidence
When I run into the house where once lived a good
                          friend of mine
The house was torn down
And then a rather more passionate continuance
Quite near the Seine and further along the Left Bank
And finally
In front of the shop of
                          one inexplicable bookseller
It is my old man
I know that this day will fulfill all my premonitions
A brief feeling of dread
But then the old man vanishes
I know I will never meet him again
Perhaps only if I were to end up in some unpredictable danger

This day in May briefly allows me to borrow
                                    the traits of a mirror
I will carry them with me even at night like a lamp
                        to capture myself during a less glorious battle

On Rue de Rivoli the evening arrives
The automobiles honk in the distance
But here the pavement trembles only from autumn memories

Once in a while, a few skirts flutter
And in my heart it feels like a blow undoubtedly
                                    caused by an echo
And that feeling within me strengthens every shadow
                            that passes through the leaves
I would like to scream.
All the scents that I gathered on this day's stroll
Transform into a buxom, bare woman
It is the daughter of the old man who bartered my brain
                            she is scorching and dashes away
And I run after her towards the underground train
She blends in with the crowd
                        exiting towards Boulevard des Italiens
And vanishes in a clothing shop
                        where the shades are lowered
The roar of the animal imprisoned in the automobile
Your roar, desire awakening once more
                            forever quenching desire
My love, my desire, my hopes, and my mirth
At last the automobile hurls me at Café de l'Univers
My final journey
While the straggling pedestrians vanish
                            from the French comedy
And sitting on a chair I drink the last aperitif of the day

The May square from which I began my quest before noon
 Grows peaceful, all so peaceful
And in two, three hours it will begin to sleep
Imaginary Marianna! It is a sedative like your orchard
The ozone above the surface of fantasy
                    when a spark vanishes and darkness comes
It is Paris that fills my brain
With a Leyden jar a thousand times discharged
And now it is peaceful as me
I who write this verse
Like the last lamp that places the period
                                    at the end of a day

To the Black Woman

A Parisian Saturday
Paradise for the midinette
At Café Weber, along the harbor of the street
Their colorful boats float in and out

When I think of you
That lengthy gamut
From Madeleine to Étoile
Never stops, never stops changing oars

Her slipper
Staccato
A golden and blue handkerchief
Fallen in the afternoon

I see trips to Versailles
And to Fountainebleau
With that pair of eyes
That are pretty as an aperitif

There is still time
For on Place Vendôm
The same silence as in a palace
Suits my rendezvous

When I think of you
Any storeroom
Offers velvet to my thoughts
For your lips, for your eyes, for your shapes

No ebony
No Carmen
Will ever compete with the moon
Turning brown on Guadeloupe

Perhaps only patina
The houses doomed for ruin
Whisper your story to me
Colored by the dresses of this season

If you would like
A meridian of chimneys
Could imitate your
Homeland and your evil
And I would follow you there

I desire you
And I am deterred
These two fateful motions
Create love

I know nothing of the Gibraltar
Growing more narrow
When your cradling arms
Try to make land out of both you and me

Coldness
You carry it with you
Like a white woman, a brown parasol
I wish to sit with you on every terrace in this world

You, who never blushes
How can I understand you?
Where can I wander and not cross the line
With my endearments and hesitations?

Unveiled flesh
The bottom of your palms is glowing coal
Do not caress me
I already have a fear of mirrors

Around Châtelet
In an attic room
I would eagerly yield to the coconut milk of your teeth
Which have opened that tropical fruit

So we would be near
The bookstores as dark as you
Like bad German romances
In those thick books
That haunt me in my dreams

And what a ride it would be
On that golden boat through that night in which you blend
Or during a moon night
Where all is white like Nice

Which muslin suited you,
Glorious creation
Who benumbs the luster of a ten-frank
Like we are benumbed by a Christmas tree?

Blend yourself in a crowd
If it is possible
You, who dresses in mourning from birth,
Like I, like those banners

Your threatening embrace
Just like a catafalque
Would bury me forever
And I no longer have the courage to live beyond the grave

Or let there be a night
That is unattainable. A shadow, chimera
And in its shapes your ebony shapes
Will find a grave and I will find your terrifying agony

The Little Flag

The white swans
At Saint-Germain des Prés
Young girls in the cafes
Love the flutter of this flag

The Café Deux Maggots
Like a looking glass
Permits me to pursue the dust of steps
Made by those blessed sixteen-year-old bodies

An angel or a Chinaman
Along the street after ten o'clock
Will sit in an automobile
Known for its make

I wouldn't be surprised
If from the church across the street
A parade of dragonflies swarmed by
And then scattered

Like a rainbow of maidens
That are painted
Like a cherry tree
Like tiny meadows
At five in the afternoon

A Farewell to Paris

The day was misty like my eyes
Mourning color clothed the skies
Grayness swelling through the haze
Like a chicken in the maize

Oh Paris, I watched you clean
The fabrics of your harlequins
In the puddles of the Seine
For you my longings never end

I recall the vivid motleys
Of your cafés and your chimneys
Your heart it has an arcane beat
like the darkness, like deceit

Mistress, your infinite intrigues
Your stories that I disbelieve
Are stronger than the truth that rests
Upon the walls of amethyst

Speak, speak deceitful one
You cunning soutane of a nun
Blather on, your stories flow
Restless like a little colt

You who simply never age
Have seen many a wrinkled face
Lovers who, while in their prime,
Foolishly would claim your time

The day was misty like my eyes
Mourning color clothed the skies
Grayness swelling through the haze
Like a chicken in the maize

Paris

Lyon

Méditerranée

P-L-M

In a shabby old train amongst bags, nets, and covers
Today was the first time I met Marseille sailors
They were blue as the fish meat and frightening as well
They brought me the sea. They carried its smell.

Something beautiful about them, stubborn in every way
They'll be the first to rebel and become captains one day
They were blue as the fish meat and frightening as well
They brought me the sea. They carried its smell.

They return to their harbor, to their regiments and rope lines
Prepared to stare harshly into their captain's bright eyes
They were blue as the fish meat and frightening as well
They brought me the sea. They carried its smell.

Some mumble and dream, others are callous and bland
As if at least once in their lives as pirates they banded
They were blue as the fish meat and frightening as well
They brought me the sea. They carried its smell.

They inhale their tobacco while in smoke they're adorned
It reminds them of the motions of a brutal ocean storm
They were blue as the fish meat and frightening as well
They brought me the sea. They carried its smell.

Young men and old have tattoos on their arms
To protect them at sea they are branded with charms
They were blue as the fish meat and frightening as well
They brought me the sea. They carried its smell.

The sea needs a man who is rugged and tough
The tougher the man, the more he fears love
They were blue as the fish meat and frightening as well
They brought me the sea. They carried its smell.

If I weren't a poet then a sailor I'd be
I fight words like a bull the way I'd fight with the sea
They were blue as the fish meat and frightening as well
They brought me the sea. They carried its smell.

I'd be the first to rebel, I'd be first on the rise
I'd gouge out those captains' pretty bright eyes
They were blue as the fish meat and frightening as well
They brought me the sea. They carried its smell.

The tenth strophe of verses to make peace in this life
I'd divorce my three-hundred-and-fifty-sixth wife
They were blue as the fish meat and frightening as well
They brought me the sea. They carried its smell.

And one last strophe just to add for the best
The future is made by those who protest
They were blue as the fish meat and frightening as well
They brought me the sea. They carried its smell.

The Abbot on the Train

Monsieur Abbot, sit for a while
In your black robe and gold chain
Don't dream of virgins on this train
Virgins are meek and men are vile

Just think of how sailors
Never leave a girl alone
Even if she's pure as snow
Monsieur Abbot, heed my words

And imagine the dilemma
If all the French virgins
Had tattoos on their skin
Where would the church hide their stigmata?

But then quite possibly
Processions of pilgrims
Would bring gifts for such virgins—
The human heart hungers for piety

Oh, Abbot and if you'd like
Take the gifts! Fill your tote
When nothing is left, just hit the road
Forgive my blasphemy, Jesus Christ

Avignon

When I arrived in Avignon
Thirty bells were ringing loud
The streets were scorching in the blaze
Like Bethlehem of bible days

Oh Avignon! Oh Avignon!
For whom do your bells ring
In those ancient castellations
Do you fear condemnation?

You once had three popes
Did they give you any hope?
You're like a miter, Avignon
Sleeping softly through this morn

A Region in Provence

Those lonely trees of Provence
Remind me of my home
Where among the mountain springs
The child in me once roamed

Children running to our table
Where did they play hide and seek?
By the ancient Roman stable
With the gentle smiling sheep

We used to smile with the goslings
Near the road by the willow trees
Provençal maidens come and sing
Of red-haired Meluzina's breeze

As Mistral sang in his native tongue
Of Mireio and his weaver maids
When death arrives and stops my lungs
Then I will have no more to say

I wish to sleep in Bohemia's Provence
In that grass with the chamomile
And drown in its sweet fragrance
Where peacefully I'd disappear

Marseille Roofs

Oh, Marseille rooftops! Who do you shelter?
Marseille, I watched your balconies
On one I saw an old wooden chair
On which a woman sat tearfully

I once loved the magic of ocean ferries
Those monuments of steel and chains
But today in the shade of elderberries
I was touched by that woman's pain

Who disappeared? For whom does she wait?
Why does she duel with the cards all alone?
Whose happiness is she willing to wager?
Did a Martha or Mary become her last foe?

Old woman forget your lost love
Let my belated train pass by
When love is broken like a porcelain dove
Just let it go! Dry the tears from your eyes

Oh Heart, drop your Sisyphean load
Love hard, but choose a lighter rock to carry
You're not as hardened as these seagulls
As this anchor. As this ocean ferry

The Coast

For six hours I traveled the coast
En route from Marseille to Monaco
When I saw the colors of the rainbow
On a bird's wing as it soared

These vast horizons are dear to me
And I found one here, my golden bird
If I could live and write my verse
In a lighthouse, down by the sea

I could capture the colorful Ibis
As it rests by the marble pond
I'd like to hunt you gray-eyed fawns
Dozing amongst the jasper stones

The Sea

I greet you Mediterranean Sea
This morning I saw your horizon
You're nothing but a wasteland to me
or a mushroom harboring poison
I greet you Mediterranean Sea

I greet you blue toadstool
Your cap repels the tropical heat
Men who taste you become fools
Oh sea, you're a wrinkled sheet
I greet you blue toadstool

I greet you peacock with a hundred tails
Your waters so cunningly whirl
Like a woman with hair too plain
Who colors her straw with curls
I greet you peacock with a hundred tails

I greet you rippling rainbow
Which storm was it that broke your bridge?
You're mended like a basket with a bow
And now you imitate an emerald gem
I greet you rippling rainbow

I greet you miniature sirens
With bright bans you tempt our kind
To dive into fields of forget-me-nots
Or into the depths of strange turquiose eyes
I greet you miniature sirens

I greet your tenderness dear ocean
You have the magic of table covers
For the mornings when bread is broken
In the shadows of our lovers
I greet your tenderness dear ocean

I greet your bitterness salty waters
You tame a brute like a falling tear
You calm the harshness of human anger
Ancient glaciers brought you here
I greet your bitterness salty waters

I greet your tongue oh Babylon
Let me taste your conflicting truths
And if I'd cast them into one
Who'd find your apocryphal root
 I greet your tongue oh Babylon

I greet your strength angry bull's eye
And I greet the bravery of the matador!
He swam out far beyond the tide
Onto the dark ocean floor
I greet your strength angry bull's eye

I greet you savage cock
I hail your sadistic and bloody fights
You tempt our children who then begin
To duel each other with all their might
I greet you savage cock

I greet you curse of King Lear
Who turned his back on Cordelia
My friends, when the time is near
Insanity too will strike me down
I greet you curse of King Lear

I greet you deep blue hurricane
Sensual passions of imagination
I greet your flaxen horse's mane
Which never yields to degradation
I greet you deep blue hurricane

I greet you painful purple cysts
Rapidly spreading from head to toe
We still feel those deadly pricks
 From poisonous mosquitoes
I greet you painful purple cysts

I greet you airy colonnade
Waging wild wars with stormy skies
I throw myself into your raids
Like an acrobat swinging high
I greet you airy colonnade

I greet you deceitful killer
A mask hides your beguiling skill
The cruelty your victim endures
Is the price a widow pays for your will
I greet you deceitful killer

I greet you lively carnival feast
Dressed to kill at your masquerade ball
Malnourished larvas become big fat beasts
Your frivolity has no end at all
I greet you lively carnival feast

I greet you daring gingerbread baker
From what tubes do you squeeze your glaze?
Your shop is like a dreamcatcher
The shepherd becomes a prince one day
I greet you daring gingerbread baker

I greet you airy ladies' lace
Garnished with a touch of folklore
Like froth at Aphrodite's birthplace
You're the veil of a dress I adore
I greet you airy ladies' lace

I greet you hysterical lady
Who dwells in her own hallucinations
Only a poet will know all your cravings
Your deceitfulness, your palpitations
I greet you hysterical lady

I greet you Mediterranean Sea
I close my eyes, there's no more to see
I recognize your fantastic grief
With its thousand eyes, its agility
I greet you Mediterranean Sea

A Ride on an Ocean Wave

A Ride on an Ocean Wave

Finally I lie upon you, ocean wave
An instant of pleasure and then you fold
All my old lovers are here today
Love hurls me to shore, love grinds me below

Then you lift me above your cunning breasts
Where silence is just a step away
Love hurles me to shore, love scythes me to death
Where the worm slithers softly to feast on its prey

The waves knock me down, again they come at me
With a short farewell and a long goodbye
When old lovers fade, I'm alone with the sea
As it lulls me to sleep on its bosoms and thighs

Oh, indolent movement! We jump over waves
We pity those who are left on the shore
The wave will destroy them. Let the lyre play
Until we are done with that oversung score

Oh, rocking motion! I place the burden
Of my words and thoughts into your arms
With a gentle passion I lean toward your surface
As I'm making circles with the touch of my palms

That ride on the waves, that ecstatic divan
Gives me visions like a hashish den
And the water's treasure, hidden so long
Falls into my hands when I open them

Beatitude makes an axis within me
I orbit around it like stars in the night
I swing in the lulls and I swing in the epics
The wave helps me conquer the holiday light

There will surely be other times, other women
Much other poetry, and still the same kiss
But I will submit, Oh spume of the ocean
If death strikes me now, I will end in your bliss

Maids of Monaco

Those bridesmaids of Monaco
Are chaperoned by old women
(Grandmothers? Who knows?)
En route to first communion

If I met them in my dreams
It would be a travesty.
Christ, they're all dressed up like brides

In their long veils and myrtle wreaths!
May their grandfathers rest in peace

Oh, beautiful maids, never grow old!
For you the bells of Monte Carlo toll

Your arms are like the palest linen
From which coffin were you stolen?

Oh, maids! I can see you trembling
As the bells in town are ringing

Le Napolitain

On the terrace in le Napolitain
Breakfast has a pleasant flow
As I listen to this Italian mumbo jumbo

Mrs. Melica shouts, "I can't take it!
You don't know these Italians!
Eduarda will break it
And that Corsican there
Has too many plans!"

He'd better give out those flyers
Down by the casino.
Do you want to get fired?
Then move it! Let's go!

Monte Carlo is bleating like a little sheep
I love the allure of these festive streets
When the couriers are packing ice
While they grumble about their lives

Oh brittle feeling! It's hard to explain
It's like having breakfast in a picture frame

Beausoleil

Let us go to Beausoleil
To smell the scent of the orange blossoms
Oh, beautiful sun! You ask me what is missing on Earth
You visit these terraces smudged with dirt
You paint its squatters, the poor, in black
They have everything except for bread
That is what's missing!
And when the world becomes shattered glass
Then there will be nothing more to regret
You can't blame the poor, the foul slums of the city
Or the poet who admires their homes turned patina
You can't blame the stolen platinum or gold
Blame the pride of those who live with no worry
Who will never understand the logic of history

Good Night

At night when I fall asleep by the open Venetian blinds
And all the water with the scent of oranges dried out
I hear the late riders dismount from their horses
Once again another beautiful day is gone
Good night, dear poet. Go capture its voices
Bring back that time and all its brightness
For I need a reason to listen to your song

Monaco Romance

Over the steep cliffs high above the sea
Beyond the growth of the cypress trees
Just past the switchback, the serpentine road
An old castle shelters the Princess of Monaco

It is not quite a castle, it's a chateau
The princess was sleeping when I walked there alone
She had ice on her temples to sooth her headache
The priest in the temple prayed for her sake

Princess, last night you had too much to drink
You simply indulged far past the brink
The guard was an angel and the night wasn't over
He took you outside, he helped you get sober

How absurd it seems, this changing of the guard
The guardsmen go home to a beach or a barge
And put on those silly operetta cockades
If you serve in the guard you're a man that is made

These walls embrace museum cannons
Yet the thrill of war has long been abandoned
Cannon balls are stacked into tiny pine trees
Under the sun they rest there in peace

Oh, republics of our modern age
This monarchy has put you to shame
It makes a mockery out of our state
Oh, republic! You have sealed your fate

Your armies and your raging guns
Should only be in museums
As well as your stocks, charters, and roulette
Perhaps when better times are met

Monaco Streets

In Monaco the flags have colorful labels
A shirt, an apron, a tablecloth
Apollinaire gave me this thought
He lived here once and imagined his fables

The withering magic of old windows
The silhouettes of muses in lace
Gave shape to his exotic taste
And that's why he adored Prague so

Perhaps he too wore a sailor's shirt
Like the children who run through Monaco
He freshened his poems with miracles
And that is why we praise his art

Oh William in heaven! I beg you please
Bring down your lyrical circus
A poet like me will never fuss
About Rembrant's gaudiness on the cheap

Surely poetry would be a bore
If it weren't for the Monaco streets
It was a bookshelf that inspired me
An old school attic with a dusty floor

Aquarium

1

Even the most powerful fantasies
Could never compete with the glass display
Where the fish of the world
Gather like words in a poet's verse

One fish—the horse
One fish—the hay
Those are only a few examples of the metaphorical courage

That nature controls
Every pond, however soiled it may be
                                    labors tenaciously
To bestow once in its life an electrical spark
Perhaps we dream in strange and special moments
                                    of our own embryonic springs
So that we mature in time to a consciousness of protozoans
Or perhaps it is the work
                        of those microscopic beings within us
An aquarium illuminated by our thoughts

2

Fish, the butterfly that has the magic Java maids
When they bathe in the sea
Bringing back a memory of the breeze
In a palace of lilies that it yields to its raids

3

Kiss that bloating bourgeois belly
His love ends with a hiccup
And floats upon the moon's beauty
Kiss that bloating bourgeois belly

4

If all the wigs in the world would come to life
Like this ghastly squirming hair
Would any one of us even dare
To seek commitment from a maiden or a wife?
Love would be a much crueler tyranny
One that we could hardly bear
We'd either be strangled in pure agony
Or love only women with no hair

5

A breathing tube
Is it not a signal that summons
The dead to their judgment day?
Intestines become balls of string
As they leave this corner of the cemetery
The soul flexes its muscles
And tears apart
those solid cliffs of basalt

6

Fingertips searching for the killer
They touch a wall and touch a home
And in this little guilty pleasure
They reach the child who sleeps alone

7

Two torn tongues caress
The waters suspiciously bend
Can love end underwater
With playfulness and more playfulness?

8

Crowns from the cockfight left behind
And the eyes of hens attached to hair
Conjure Erinys's body in this sky
Blood is still gushing, blood is pouring everywhere

9

Ask me what is the purpose of these colorful patterns
Produced by either insanity or by another more ideal
                                                life form
Ask why we are drawn and enticed
                              by all that is absurd and unknown
There will be a time when it no longer overwhelms us
                                        when all will be known
Ask my fantasy why it wallows in barren
                          places with overgrown bushes and moss
Ask me and I will not explain
Why nature could not create only one breed of beings
It would have been simpler

And yet it is above all exciting when there is no logic
when in that moment all is forefeit

And why shouldn't poetry
Have the same reason to exist
                    as an aquarium?

Promenade des
Anglais

Cactuses

When men restrict their bodies
The human race begins to dwarf
Men die out in the shade of a robe
Oh lilliputian cactuses, behold!

A woman loses beauty but she is still kind
Her saggy embrace fears the thought of a giant
She grows tiny cactuses on her windowsill
She no longer breeds, she doesn't have the will

As seasons pass we lose our fantasies
Soon even a snake will be difficult to see
And then we'll yearn from time to time
For all those wild stone-age vines

I have seen cactuses that flourish in the tropics
I'd like to speak of apes, a rather peculiar topic
In their shadows humans are a minuscule race
Size has a conscience and size has a face

Imagine trees that look like spoons
Trees that resemble fish-eating loons
Imagine a cactus with the head of a lamb
A clock-like cactus without a minute hand

A cactus crinkled like a hunter's horn
A cactus waving good bye with its thorns
A cactus crispate, like a human head
A cactus without arms, a cactus without legs

A cactus jolting like skeleton bones
A cactus with epaulettes commanding its zone
A cactus with a fish spine, fleshless and withered
A cactus dipped in a bowl full of feathers

Since humans learned to live with each other
Nature, your imagination has seemed to falter
I'm grateful for the bit I can still adore
Strange cactuses, have I seen you before?

Villefranche

The naval harbor of Villefranche
Brightly painted like an orange
A multicolored merchant fleet
Takes its market to the sea

And in the narrow dirty lanes
On the barrels children dream
Lovers hold each other's hands
Through the windows across the street

And when I dive into the sea
I think it might devour me
And suddenly my soul grows stripes
A captain's shirt in blue and white

Promenade des Anglais

I see the marble shore through my dark glasses
And the most beautiful women in the world
Sit here in wicker chairs as time
                                    pleasantly passes
A parasol becomes a flower that multiplies
And your white palaces
Offer the sun a touch of ice
As backstage
Pendulous bedrooms sway from left to right
Oh English Promenade
You adulteress garnished with jewels and light
I know your heart is foul
But your embrace is pure as a crystal band
That lets me forget you're a thousand times damned
And in your white inkwell I dip my pens
You're a plate on which Rio glistens

Old Nice

This latrine for princesses and their servants
Is decorated with pornographic scenes
She is the lowest of her kin
A beautified harlot, but she's far too lean

And yet her legs can hold balconies
And crooked manger gates
Still, you want to glance at her
And open this foul-smelling crate

Filled with cheap trinkets like a knackery
Soon you'll ignore the mange of her streets
Oh harlot, only Rembrandt can match your beauty
I'll trade my cobalt for your filth in a heartbeat

Gunshots

When I passed through Nice I stopped in Cimiez
Where in its empty gardens and villas
The water in the swimming pools had turned green
But there were enough roses to cover the stench
Capitalism decayed in the breeze of their scent
The hotels were haunted and the villas were closed
Opulence without people turned buildings into ghosts
I felt as if I had stumbled on Pompeii
Even the echoes of my footstep frightened me that day

Beyond the last house I spotted a monastery
It slept like a cherub in a garden by a cemetery
I walked past the graves for the aristocracy
Like Cimiez they were lifeless, yet they were full of beauty
Old wreaths were withered along with their bows
Like Herculaneum in the sad ruins of rainbows

I walked to a banister, I took in the scenery
A peaceful mass had ended in that old monastery
I heard shots in the air as I was dozing off
I woke up and wondered: was I being robbed?

Before I came to, I heard a second round of guns
As if thirty churches slammed their doors at once
I though I was delirious in the subtropical heat
Then I saw the army barracks just down the street

Never have I seen my epoch this close
Like in Cimiez that day in a breeze of roses
What good is the beauty of a distant shore
When soldiers are training for a more horrific war?
I decided to retreat, I didn't wish to stay

Then I read a little sign on the monastery's gate
Its letters glistened as if they were magical
With words that beckoned me: Be kind to animals.

Oh, this should be the motto for all those in power
That time will come to mark their last hours
Around the rose bushes we'll watch our children
Laughing and playing in these beautiful gardens

Children of workers have suffered the most
There'll be no more haunting, no signs of ghosts
When that famous day comes then revenge will be sweet
So be kind to animals! Oh, be kind to revolutionaries!

Cannes

This fine Saturday in Cannes
Is what a spring depot could be like
Shopkeepers waving all around
Like a church flag raised up high

In the harbor below a fort
Of window blinds and pleasant roofs
Ships with cargo of exotic sorts
Quietly smoke, a bit aloof

The captain peacefully tokes his pipe
Oh ferries! Avoid a stormy night
Don't hit a mine upon the sea
If Angelus in Cannes rings a shipbell
Then all my happiness will end as well
Like poetry going up a chimney

Saint-Honorat

There is a monastery with a cross,
On the island of Saint-Honorat
Go and see it then, you must
Climb its tower to the top

The monks they have their Christus Venit
In the matutinum of time
When they clear their morning spit
Of the taste of smoke and wine

Which they drank in their cellar
With toothsome fish, pâté, and beef
Still renouncing every fortune
Devouring this holy feast

You too would salivate
Over a turkey platter
Given a barrel of tasty mead
You'd summon Satan after

Satan dressed in a black robe
With a wine carafe in his arms
Or perhaps you would sadly go
 Back to that famished city of Cannes

Île Sainte-Marguerite

The Island of Saint Margaret
Is rather overgrown with moss
Like my old aunts' flowerbed
Where we would play in the grass

Where is the love? I ask
For the great marshal Bazin
Henri in his steel mask
Knelt here to redeem his sins

On these stones in this dungeon cell
Then he was taken to the Bastille
Was it here that he heard nightingales?
Or perhaps they were never real

Oh beautiful marshal's lady
Where has your lover strayed?
He jumped and swam across the sea
And a ship took him away

Your rendezvous are at their end
You'll be a missus once again
How thrilling it was to hide
A conspirer's letter at your side

You'll never fall in love again
With your marshal, young and brave
In idleness you'll meet your end
On an empty promenade

You'll never be back on this island
That boat from Cannes you'll never take
You'll have children, you'll have a husband
A home, boredom, and fear of heartbreak

Who will remove your steel mask?
If only you could come to me
To you I'd proclaim my love at last
Kneeling on nettles upon my knees

It's a shame we no longer live
In the time of great romance novels
We'd share a bunk in the prison cell
Of one honorable marshal

Come along, we both could marvel
I don't say this out of jest
On a motorcycle we could travel
Dinner in Antibes would be the best

Then we would drink a little
A dance, jazz, a masquerade
Perhaps you'd find it magical
As I find your legend today

La Turbie

On the back of a giant camel
Amongst the antique dust and gravel
A city with pillars built by Augustus
And a church in the shade of cypresses

How great it is to watch the sea!
In a coop the chickens feed
It's intimate and you feel like home
As if you read a perfect poem

The children have been told to sweep
Droppings off these ancient streets
I'm sitting in the low-cut grass
Am I in Moravia at last?

This ancient Roman Saturday
Brings memories of a hard life
You await the rumble in Turbie
On Saturday's merchants' derby

Menton

It was in the little town of Menton
By an old church right before noon
The courtyard of the local sexton
Was scattered with antique heirlooms

It was there I bid farewell to France
Where grace blended together with love
The hour and the minute hands
Told me it was over, my time was up

Enough, you artist of plein-air eras
It's time to preach on your native land
Its time to abandon that pathetic opera
And search beyond your limited wingspan

Beyond the chimneys, gutters, and sparrows
Beyond the walls cleansed by the rain
Forget the abstract and aim your arrows
To a place where poetry can seize its reins

Poetry gushing from the knowledge of life
From its ordinary and fantastic ways
And by a fence it too can thrive
Where the houseleek with the carline plays

Poetry beyond messianism
Or sublimity and its heavy pace
Oh Bohemia, France offers you
Its Roman eyes, its Gaullish grace

Czech poets release the light
The inner child of your heroes
Let them shout with all their might
Colorful life, I love you so!

On an Italian Train

Ventimiglia

In Ventimiglia as soon as I arrived
After farewells to France and all its spires
The fascist regime and its dismal attire
Clothed in mourning, my free will deprived

I once dreamed of Italy in my sleep
As I dreamed of Goethe's beloved Mignon
And now it's an airplane I'd rather be on
To fly from those who buried it deep

Pretty brunette—what a shame, what a waste
Your brown eyes have been covered in dirt
Covered by Mussolini and his black shirts
And the night has many diamonds for grace

They are Sabina's tears hardened to the core
She's ashamed to look upon this land
Where hordes of locusts have come to band
Under the box tree to trill a song of war

On an Italian Train

This Italian train is a lasting nuisance
The feeling of war waits in the distance
Italian soldiers covered in grime
All over the trains, all of the time

Oh sea, what burden you bear
Oh starry night, extinguish your flare
Sorrow has taken hold of me

How should I hide my bloodshot eyes?
I know, I'll ride through Italy
With my eyes closed so I don't have to see

The Walls in Genoa

The Genoa walls pose their elephant skin
Decorated in vulgar phrases
I love those brittle coulisses
And that theatrical paper rose
I can find them in the trash at the midnight hour
With remnants of lamp beams and remnants of flowers
Christopher discovers under a pot lid
Another new world guarded by spiders

A Sweeping View of Milan

An exhibit of rose-colored canvases
Beneath the sky upon the flatland
The Siena mud fired like the sun
Why, those are the rooftops of Milan!
The morning twilight crushed into clay
Oh sun! Feast on them with your rays

Romeo and Juliet

Near Desenzano
Is Garda lake
Early on the morrow
Gently I wake

Along the Italian platform
With its playful persona
Oh, silent song
I sleep through Verona

The train passes through
A lake of bouquets
And suddenly I remember
My uncle's young days

Then that lonely stone grave
Where the flowers have dried
I'm so sorry, dear uncle
That you marched and you died

Oh, Austrian fellow
They captured your regiment
On a foreign meadow
You slept in a tent

You woke with the horses
To a sky without blue
You wrote your own verses
Just like your nephew

Venice

Venice! How can I describe you?
How do I open your whimsical vial
Are you a city of gaudiness or style?
An ancient landau? A widow or a bride?

Oh étagère! I don't like your annals!
The tombs where your doges mold
I prefer your coffins made of gold
As they rock upon your channels

I love your portals and your bowers
Where for a lira one can dream
Possessions flow here like a stream
Through the hollow of a mirror

Your streets are like ancient wardrobes
For castaway dreams and hats
Where local children play with cats
And crabs that the girls carry home.

Is this a block or a two-story barge
With a chimney turned outside in?
Hours fly by along with the pigeons
And the archangel of Saint Mark's

Oh ciboriums, you golden altars
Your grandeurs no longer amaze
I'm in a labyrinth of mirrored mazes
In a dream book that a gypsy barters

Venice, you're grimy like that gypsy's face
With earrings shaped like rosebuds
Filthy like the miracle of mud
Like her sunken and sleepy grace

Rachelle

I'm just too tired, Rachelle,
But we'll make do on this narrow bench
Take my hand and go to sleep
We might as well be friends

I'm just too tired, Rachelle,
And soon you'll ride another train
Sleep childlike, deathlike on this bench
Our time was not in vain

I'm just too tired, Rachelle
Like your ancient villified race
Like my aging cathedral bells
Like poetry, like grace

Like laughter and like hell
I'm just too tired, Rachelle

The Return Home

The Return Home

1

In the beautiful month of May
When the world begins to bloom
Smitten by lands far away
I'll return home very soon

Where all speak with lips well known
Like the lips of a mistress lover
And tomorrow in my home
My birthday will be honored

I'll stroll my garden for a while
Where a dream lies in the sun
I'm anxious like a little child
For this precious day to come

Thirty-three years have passed in time
The stork dropped me at the start
He placed a flower in my wine
And a talon upon my heart

It remains embedded to this day
Piercing me each break of dawn
Lilacs spread their soothing ways
Upon my wound with healing balms

Some folks hide in a smile
But are tortured by guilt within

Without a purpose I tend to cry
Not knowing if I've sinned

I often shed that bitter water
Like sweetness sheds from a honeybee
I laugh for no other reason
Than this world that I see

2

In the beautiful month of May
I feel a panic all over
Smitten by lands far away
Alas, I crossed the border

This homecoming I don't regret
Or look forward to it either
Just a sigh and a deep breath
And everything will feel better

The trains are changing in Breslau
But my train has been standing still
I should have gotten off by now
I'll journey till I get my fill

3

Farewell, distances far beyond
Farewell, magic of express trains
In a local car I'll travel on
And tearfully admit my pain

The compartment seems so narrow
The train cradles and creaks away
And boyishly its whistles blow
Passing schools along the way

Someone argues close by
As always the conductor complains
Why are my anger and my pride
Fading like the drying rain?

I'm happy in this old compartment
Worn out as my bedroom chest
A granny snores and seems content
Like a village at its best

There's milk in a canister
From which I'd like to drink
The conductor might seem sinister
But he doffs his hat and winks

4

I travel through that blooming Hanau
I hide my sadness deep within
And lilacs growing all around
The Chapels for the Virgin

Some folks hide behind a smile
But are tortured by guilt within
Without a reason I tend to cry
Not knowing all my sins

I often shed that bitter water
Like a mother sheds her blood
I laugh for no other reason
My tongue sings on native mud

5

So they announced that I am home
Time flies here at my journey's end
But all I hear are words unknown
It must be you, my foreign friend

And in your proud Babylon
I feel a panic beyond its walls
My tongue of colors and of tones
Tells you nothing, nothing at all

Are you not of the human race?
Is your native tongue a lie?
Come and sing, with all your grace
And I'll sing with no reason why

Farewell and a Handkerchief

Farewell, and if we no longer meet
Our time was marvelous—we've shared enough
Farewell, and soon our trysts will be
With someone new, someone else's love

Our time was marvelous but all things end
Be silent knell your sorrow is quite clear
A kiss, a handkerchief, a ship's bell, a siren
One last smile as we part from here

Farewell and if we never speak again
Let a small memory of us unfold
Lighter than a handkerchief fluttering in the wind
Tempting as the scent of gleaming gold

And if I've seen what no one's seen before
That's for the best. Swallow, seek your native barn!
You've shown me the south where you'll nest once more
Your destiny's flight, my destiny's song

Farewell, and if it's for the last time
So much for my hopes—nothing else is left
But if you wish to meet again, don't say goodbye
Leave it to fate! Farewell and a handkerchief!

About the Author

Czech poet and playwright Vítězslav Nezval was one of the most prolific writers of the twentieth-century avant-garde. He was a leading founder of the Czech movement Devětsil (Nine Forces), a group that included luminaries such as Russian linguist Roman Jakobson and Nobel laureate Jaroslav Seifert, and which evolved into the Czech Surrealist Group. He was born in 1900 in Biskoupky, a small town in southern Moravia. In addition to this volume, his other works available in English include *The Absolute Gravedigger* (Twisted Spoon Press, 2016), *Prague with Fingers of Rain* (Bloodaxe Books Ltd., 2009), *Valerie and Her Week of Wonders* (Twisted Spoon Press, 2005), and *Antilyrik and Other Poems* (Green Integer, 2001). He died in 1958.

About the Translator

Roman Kostovski has a B.A. in Russian Language and International Relations from the College of William and Mary, and an M.A. in Russian Language and Linguistics from the University of Maryland. He also holds a Lecturer of Czech Certification from Charles University in Prague, and has taught Czech at George Washington University. He translates poetry and prose into English from Bosnian, Bulgarian, Croatian, Czech, Macedonian, Russian, Serbian, and Slovak. His translations have appeared in numerous journals, including *Absinthe-New European Writings* and *Watchword Press*. His translation of Arnost Lustig's *Porgess* was published by Northwestern University Press in 2006, and his translation of Viktor Dyk's Czech classic *The Ratcatcher* was published by Plamen Press in 2014. He has also tranlsated the poetry of Karel Kryl and Jaromir Nohavica in an album collection of songs titled *Steel Strings and Iron Curtains* (Plamen Press, 2019). In 2017, he was awarded a National Endowments of the Arts Literary Translation Fellowship.

www.ingramcontent.com/pod-product-compliance
Lightning Source LLC
Chambersburg PA
CBHW031117020726

47495CB00007B/2242